SARGENT

1856 – 1925

BY T. MARTIN WOOD

PLATE I.—LORD RIBBLESDALE

(In the collection of Lord Ribblesdale)

A portrait of the author of "The Queen's Hounds and Stag-hunting Recollections": esteemed one of the finest of Sargent's works.

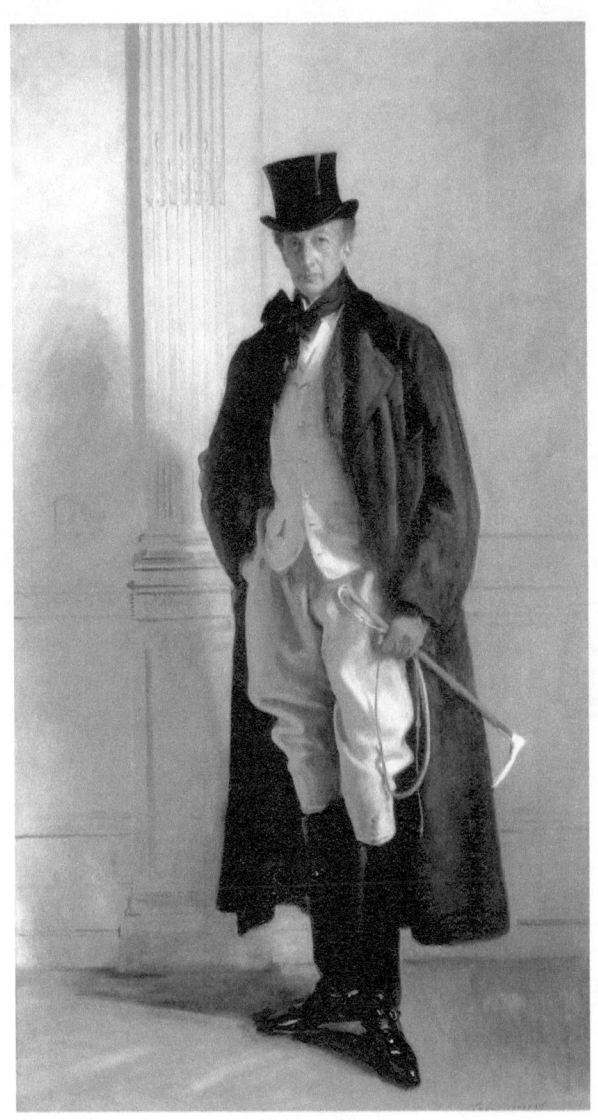

iii

ISBN-13:   978-1-0733-3928-0
ISBN-10:   1-0733-3928-9

2 4 6 8 10 9 7 5 3 1

LIST OF ILLUSTRATIONS

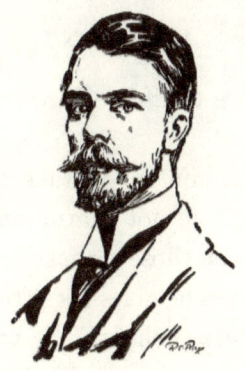

I

WAS there ever a more romantic time than our own, or a people who took everything more matter-of-factly? The paintings of a period contain all its enthusiasms and illusions. We remember the eighteenth century—at least in England—by Reynolds' and Gainsborough's art, the seventeenth century by Van Dyck's; and when we remember the eighteenth century in France, it is to think of Watteau, who expressed what his world, drifting towards disaster, cared about— an illusion of a never-ending summer's day. These names are expressive of their times, and Sargent's art, with disillusioned outlook, mirrors an obvious aspect of English life to-day. Above all others he has taken his world as it is, with the delight in life, in its everyday appearance, with which the representative artists of any period have been gifted.

Perhaps the next generation will feel that it owes more to him than to any painter of this time. For the ephemeralities of the moment in costume and fashion are the blossoms in which life seeks expression—whatever its fruit. It is agreed that everything is expression, from a spring bud bursting to a ribbon worn for a moment against a woman's hair. And who deals with the surface of life deals with realities, for the rest is guess-work.

Often enough this content to take the world as it is may result in things which do not charm us, and perhaps Sargent has never been one of those as fastidious in selection as in delineation. Sometimes he gives his sitters away—for there are traits in human nature, belief in the very existence of which we are always anxious to forego. Nothing escapes him that is written in the face. Yet he is not cynical, but man of the world, the felicity of living in a world where everything is charming being only for those with the gift to live in one of their own making.

The side of life which he expresses is that in which time seems given over wholly to social amenities, long afternoons spent in pleasant intercourse, hours well ordered and protected, so that the most fragrant qualities in human nature can if they will spring to life. We almost hear the teacups in the other room, and none of his sitters seem really alone. We feel they have left the life to which they belong to sit to the artist but only for an hour or so. The social world to which they belong will absorb them again. This world Sargent paints. Even in many of his single figures we are conscious always of its existence in the background. In portrait after portrait there is scarcely a suggestion of self-consciousness—but the man or the woman just at the moment of posing, as if environed still in an atmosphere of their own, and of the world from which they have withdrawn for the sitting. For it is Sargent's gift to remove the impression that his sitter has posed, that the dress was arranged, and his gift to arrest his sitter's habitual gesture, the impression of sparkling stones, almost the clink of bangles at the wrist in expression of the moment. Most unjustly was it said that he could not paint pretty women. It would appear to be within his power to paint almost anything that has its existence in fact, and if in a matter-of-fact way, what more to the point if the facts are so beautiful that fancy itself would have to defer?

Supreme is the art of Sargent in its appreciation of those pleasures which would almost seem for art alone: pearls upon the colour of flesh; slight transitions of colour charged with great secrets of beauty; pearls painted as they would be regarded by a lover, as ten thousand times more beautiful than if they were lying in a box. And the touches of the brush—for Sargent shows every touch—breathe sympathy with every change of colour as the chain of pearls falls first across white silk and then across black velvet, and the little globes take to themselves new variations. A fan is opened, and upon the ivory sticks the light like silver trembles, a web of colour is spun across upon the open ribs; a book is half-open, it may be a Bradshaw, but we will believe it is a book of old verse, for everything that comes into the picture, the particular picture of which I am thinking, comes into a charmed circle. There are people for whom the opulent world of Sargent's art is their everyday world—whose life competes with the splendour of day-dreams. How essentially romantic—although so matter-of-fact—must be the art that leaves us with this impression! To be matter-of-fact is, we see, far from being unromantic; the reverse indeed is true, for with our face turned from the world romance vanishes.

PLATE II.—LA CARMENCITA

(In the Luxembourg, Paris)

Painting of a Spanish Dancer. Exhibited at the Royal Academy in 1891; acquired by the French Government.

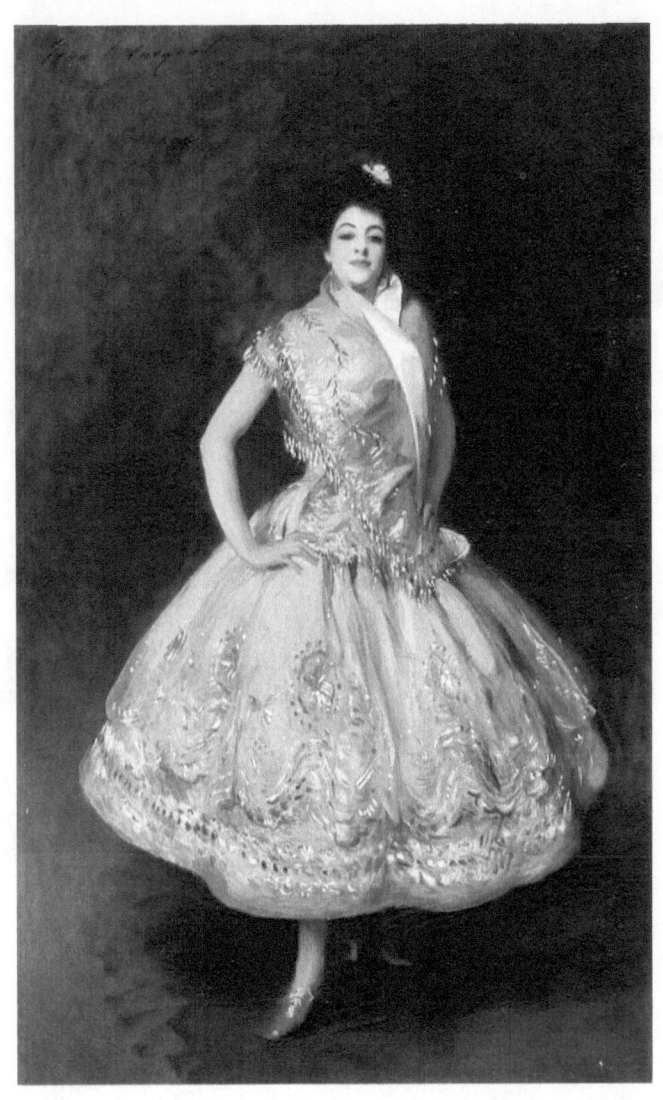

11

II

I once had occasion to call on Mr. Sargent, and was shown into a room with a black carpet. Only a colourist loves black, and sees it as a colour. And this room, so free from all that was novel and without associations, helped to explain to me why, though his method is so modern and of the moment, his pictures of aristocrats accommodate themselves to ancestral surroundings. For it is true that not only the face and the clothes of his sitters are given, but somehow, in the material of paint, their social position and their distinction. Now this is not by any means the least of Sargent's qualities; it is not a common one. Well-bred people drive up to the door of a modern studio almost visibly cloaked in the traditions of their race, but we are led to believe that they must have left all this behind them in the carriage when we see the portrait in an exhibition; the artist has shown nothing of it, has used his distinguished sitter simply as a model. For lack of inspiration novelties are proffered in its place, *L'art nouveau* on canvas. Sargent does not paint modern people as if they all came into the world yesterday landed from an airship. No, he is like Van Dyck, who not only painted the beautiful clothes, the long white hands, and the bearing of his sitters sympathetically, but also the very atmosphere of the Court around them, painting, as all great painters do, invisible as well as visible things. If there is not in Sargent's painting courtesy of touch, if his method has not suavity in painting elegant people, this is rather as it should be in an age which trusts implicitly to the dressmaker and tailor for its elegance. And without a word here as to the worth of some of our modern aims, at least the age is too much in earnest for a pose. The poses and fripperies of the pictures of Van Dyck and Kneller are done with; and besides, the modern baronet is not anxious to show his hands, but is painted gloved, and Work goes unimmortalised. Meunier the sculptor and other modern artists having gloried in the war of labour, its victories go unsung; its victors surviving only as fashionable men.

The portraits of some painters suggest nothing but the foreign atmosphere of a studio, but Sargent seems to meet his sitters in the atmosphere of their own daily, fashionable life, and that is why his pictures are romantic, for isn't there romance wherever there is wealth? The people whose wealth is such that they can take as their own background all the beautiful accessories of aristocratic tradition, are entitled to them if they like them well enough to spend their money in this way. And it is the peculiar gift of our age to recognise in ourselves the heirs of the centuries of beautiful handicrafts, which we close with our machines. They certainly are the heirs to any kind of beauty who have the imagination to enjoy it. And the imagination for past associations, who have this more than the Americans? We believe in England that all Americans are rich, that they can buy whatever they appreciate. So by the divine right of things going to those who appreciate them, the rich American is now, even as Sargent paints him, environed by old French and English things and their associations. And in connection with the accessories in Sargent's pictures, might we not ask the question whether it could not be considered a test of the worth or worthlessness, from a point of beauty, of any ornament or furniture whether it would survive representation in a picture? How much modern stuff we should have to sweep aside! And now that one thinks of it, modern pictures have left modern furniture rather severely alone—the painters have not been faithful to their brethren the makers of modern tables and chairs. Who is more modern than Sargent—and I am trying to think has he ever painted a modern room—that is, a room with modern things in it? The rooms that the most modern people live in are oddly enough the ones that are most old-fashioned, filled with eighteenth-century things. This, to reflect upon, has arisen through thinking about Sargent's interior paintings, which so very vividly and accurately reflect the attitude of the modern world to its own time. In that word modern, if we are not using it too often, we must seek the nature of Sargent's painting, its spirit; it is the most interesting thing in connection with painting to come as close as possible to its spirit. And what a test before any work of art, to ask whether it is worth a search for the incorporeal element; although in vain, in spite of Walter Pater, does painting aspire "towards the condition of music," since music is as ghostly as the ghosts that it contains.

PLATE III.—ELLEN TERRY AS "LADY MACBETH"

(In the National Gallery, Millbank)

A portrait of Miss Ellen Terry purchased from the Sir Henry Irving Sale at Christie's in 1907, and presented to the nation by the late Sir Jos. Duveen, who also bequeathed a sum of money for the erection of the Turner Room now being added to the National Gallery at Millbank.

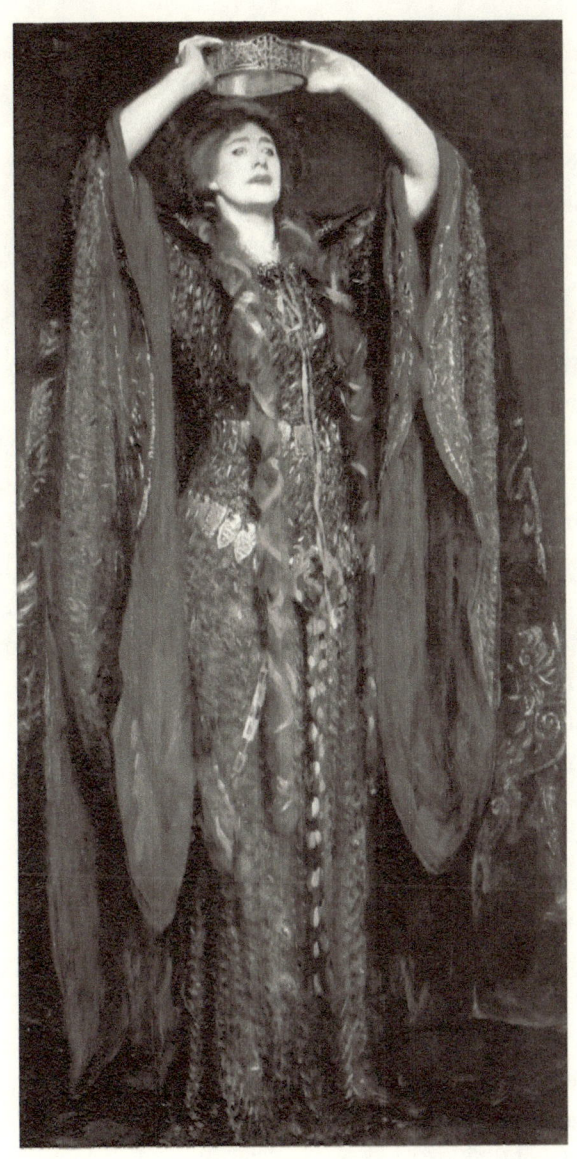

III

DANCING has been a theme always appealing to artists because of its rhythm, its grace in reality, its incarnation of femininity. It contains all the inspiration for a painter in any one moment of movement. No two things could be further removed from each other than Lancret's "La Camargo Dansant" and Sargent's "Carmencita," yet some alliterative resemblance in the name and some resemblance in the dancers' costumes bring these two figures together in my mind—the one the fairy artificial dancer, the princess of an unreal world, the other a vivid sinuous presentment. With both painters the costume has interested them as much almost as the figure, for the dress of a dancer, indeed the dress of any woman, is in a Sargent picture a part of herself, nothing mere dead matter, everything expressive, the brush having come at once to the secret that no one material thing is more spiritual than another. For ever Carmencita stands, waiting for the beginning of the music, just as La Camargo is caught upon the wing of movement, seeming to revive the music that was played for her and cheating us with a sense of a world happier than it is. In Carmencita we have that living beauty from which, after all, a dreamer must take every one of his dreams. It is Sargent's wisdom to stand thus close to life. In the sense of this reality, and the difficulty of approach to it with anything so constitutionally artificial as a painter's colours, do we apprise the real nature of his gifts. The roses on La Camargo's dress are artificial roses, but not more artificial than her face and hands. This figure is only a little nearer to nature than a china shepherdess, it is the fancy of a mind cheating itself with unrealities as realities. Sargent himself has painted artificial things, the rouge on lips, the powder on a face; since it is natural for some folk to rouge, that is the nature which he paints. Only an imaginative woman makes herself up. A painter with more imagination than Sargent would enter into the spirit of her arts. Sargent's betrayal of his fashionable sitters has frightened many, but if anything it has increased his vogue; for above everything an imaginative woman is curious to know what she looks like to others, and a Sargent's portrait is intimate, unflattering, perfectly candid but perfectly true as an answer to her question.

Everything on the stage is artificial; what will this art, that has had of the reality of things all its strength and life, make of a purely theatrical picture—Miss Ellen Terry in a famous part? The artificiality of the stage always presents two aspects, that one in which we forget its artificiality and that other in which we remember it. And this latter, to my mind, is the aspect in which Sargent has painted this picture, without, as it were, ever stepping over the footlights into the world that only becomes real on the other side of them. But the exactness of his interpretation beautifully explains the scene.

"Carnation Lily, Lily Rose" was painted in a garden by the Thames. Two children are lighting up the Chinese lanterns, and in their light and with flowers surrounding, Sargent sees for a moment life itself by accident made idyllic. The picture is Japanese in its sense of decoration, as if decoration and idyllic moments always went together. It would almost seem so from the study of art, for without exception, those painters who have been conscious of the ideal and idyllic element in life, have always shown this through composition which, whilst dealing with a real scene, has taken a little of the reality from it. There must be an essentially musical element in the art which takes a mood as well as a scene from nature, and brings us by way of real scenes to that imaginative country which exists in every nature-lover's mind; a country partly made up of the remembrance of other places which have been like the place where he now stands.

Great tiger-lilies hang over the children. We almost expect in these surroundings pierettes or fantastic lovers, but we are kept close to the beauty of reality by the naturalism with which the children have been painted. Not one touch is given as a concession to their fairy and dramatic background, not one ribbon, nothing in the costume to enable them to enter into the patterned world of art as part of a design. For above everything the painter has wished to persuade us of life itself as a picture, and not of his ability to make these children the motifs of design. Their ordinariness irritates me personally, they do not seem quite to belong to their fairy land, but I recognise that this matter-of-factness peculiarly belongs to Sargent's art and am interested in the attitude that takes beauty so matter-of-factly.

IV

NO one has encountered the beauty of woman's face more casually than Sargent, no one has made us realise more fully its significance as a fact in the world. After all we had thought perhaps we were partly deceived in this matter by the illusions of poets and love-sick painters, but approaching it without ecstasy, art has not been closer to this beauty than here. I am looking at a half-tone reproduction of a lady by Sargent, wondering whether in the history of English portrait painting an artist has approached as closely to the thoughts of his sitter. The expression of the face is determined partly by thoughts within, partly by light without. And it is as if with the touch of a brush a thought could be intercepted as it passed the lips. This is the nearest approach that thought has ever had to material definition. Thought is the architect of her expression, by accuracy of painting it is copied, just as the back of a fan or bracelet is copied—things so material as that. So after all thoughts are not so far away from the material world with which we are in touch; are scarcely less visible than air. The impressionists have rendered air; and would it be too far-fetched to hint that the shadow on the lips almost serves to bridge one province with another, the atmosphere without and that which reigns within the sitter's mind. It is when Sargent's brush hesitates at the lips and eyes, at the threshold of intimate revelation, that we really begin to form an adequate conception of his genius. Yes, of things fleeting, a thought flitting across the face, interrupted gestures—and the mysterious suggestion of conversation hanging fire between the sitter and ourself, Sargent is the master. Sometimes a portrait painter will create a face on canvas, of pleasant expression, which is not like his sitter, and it is as if with every touch he could change the thoughts as he changes the expression in the face he is creating.

Sargent's accuracy is such that the expression that passes over the face in his portraits is one which all the sitter's friends recognise; so close is he in touch with the delicate drawing, especially round the lips, that his brush never strays by one little bit into the realm of invention. There are other painters painting as carefully, faces as full of expression, who do not come near a likeness of their sitter. In what provinces close to nature are they wandering, since, striving to paint the face before them, they paint another face? We must not forget, in thinking of Sargent's greatness, that he unfailingly is in close touch with his sitters' expression, that is, almost with their thoughts.

Although Sargent has proved in many landscapes his powers in that direction, he too well enters into the spirit of the portraiture to which he has put his hand to attempt to introduce naturalistic effects into backgrounds obviously painted in a London studio. The landscape background is sometimes charming if under these circumstances it remains a convention; for there are moments when nature herself is out of place, pictures in which human nature must be the only form of life,— with the exception perhaps of flowers, for these accompany human nature always, to revelries where sunlight is excluded, and even to the tomb. It is art of little carrying power that is exhausted upon some transcript of beautiful detail, colour of the glazes of a vase, a bunch of flowers. Sargent embraces difficulties one after another with energy unexpended. Physique,

PLATE IV.—W. GRAHAM ROBERTSON, ESQ.

(In the collection of W. Graham Robertson, Esq.)

A portrait of the writer of the children's play "Pinkie and the Fairies" and many charming children's books illustrated by their author, himself an artist of high attainment.

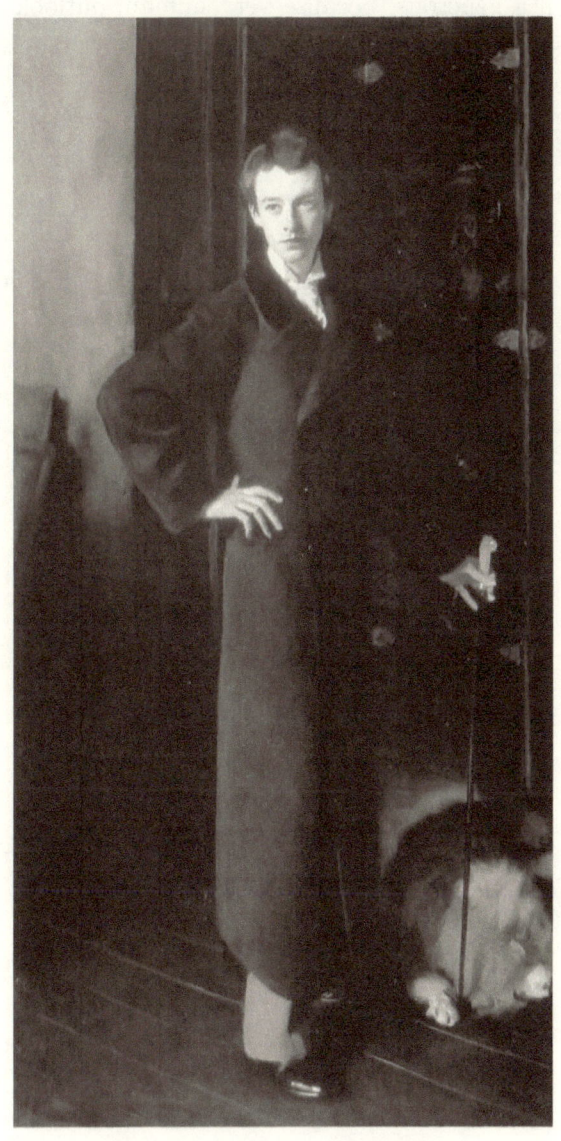

but never genius will give out. Energy of this order always goes with a generous, because very human, outlook; success on occasion being modified not through failure to accomplish, but through failure to respond.

V

THE life of a busy portrait painter, with its demand for inspiration every morning, is of the most exacting nature, and the quality of the painter's output must of necessity vary. The nervous strain is great, for sitters are capricious, and always is the temptation present to the one sin that is unforgivable, compromise with the Philistine—the concession of genius to stupidity, of perceptions nearly divine to ignorance. Genius has always had difficulty in working to order, yet nearly all the great portraiture work in the world has been done to order. But one imagines that the conditions under which the masterpieces of a modern painter, with so great a vogue as Sargent's, have been produced must be unparalleled by anything in the history of ancient painting. A crowd streamed through the studios of Gainsborough, Reynolds, and Romney to be painted, but the world was smaller then, and their art was more easily done. They worked within a convention narrower than Sargent's, compromising with nature at the very start; a convention more beautiful than his, a garden, beautiful because it was confined and seen in an accustomed light. If things are beautiful at all they become more so when they are no longer unaccustomed, when they fit in with an old frame of mind. Sargent deals with the unaccustomed—in which at first perhaps we always see the ugly—whilst, as we have said, he does not destroy, as the vandalistic art of some painters does, the connection between the past and present. It is the present which his art embraces, but we might almost say we are never thoroughly accustomed to the present until it has become the past. So to us Sargent's art is not as beautiful as Gainsborough's, for it has constantly to throw over some old form of perfection to embrace a new difficulty. In the eighteenth century there was less variety in the life which art encountered. The life of even a Gainsborough or a Reynolds would be circumscribed in just the same way that their art is circumscribed, uninterrupted in its mood, and beauty is to be found in uninterrupted moods.

PLATE V.—CARNATION LILY, LILY ROSE

(In the National Gallery, Millbank)

This painting was bought for the nation under the terms of the Chantrey Bequest in 1887, seven years previous to the painter's election to associateship of the Royal Academy.

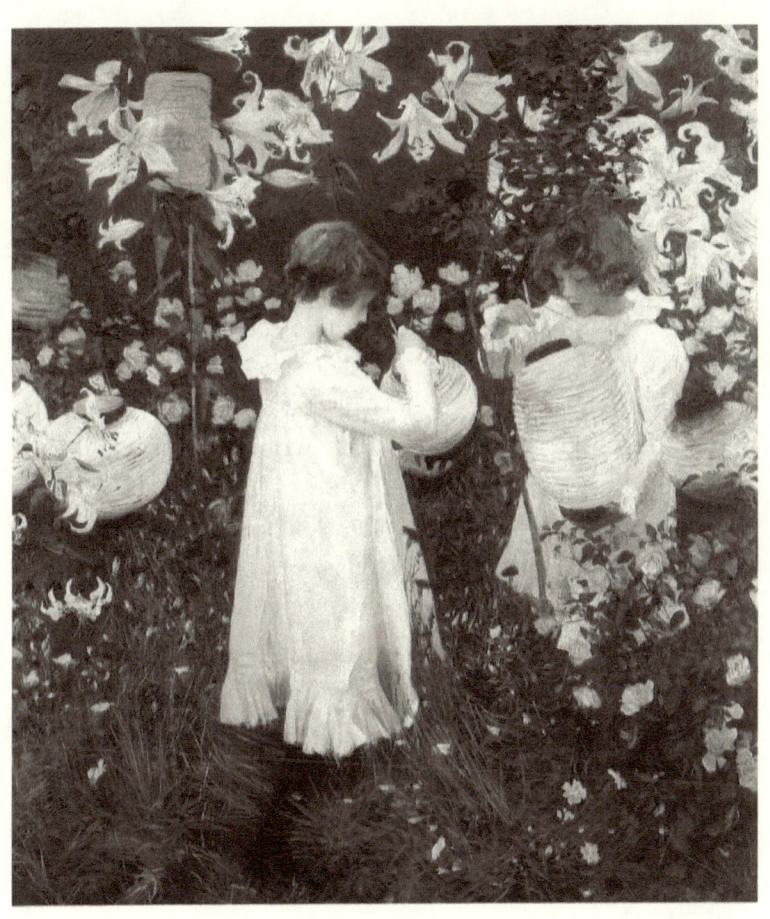

VI

SOMETHING should now be said of Sargent's method—of that which is spoken of as his technique. And of method, it is not something to be separated from the painter's temperament, it is always autographic. Somehow, temperament shows even in a person's handwriting, giving it what is really its style, though the fashion of writing imposed upon a pupil by his master is also called a style. In art there is no word that is oftener debated. And of those who speak most of style in their own work, the measure of their self-consciousness in the matter is often the measure of their distance from it. They are in the position of a schoolboy taking writing lessons, and their style, if ever they are to have one, does not begin until thinking and painting have become for them almost one process. But this is a difficult matter to make clear, and apology should perhaps be forthcoming for touching on so debatable a point thus hurriedly. I may have said something perhaps to convey to the lay reader the significance of the particular method of treating his subjects which we identify with Sargent. The pupil of Carolus Duran, his method was formed under the most modern influences; whatever effect quite another kind of training might have had on Sargent, still nothing but the traceable element of self would have determined for us his style. The method of applying paint to canvas has always resolved itself into more or less a personal question, though certain schools are to be identified with different ways of seeing; every method is a convention, and the difference of conventions always one of vision, affecting handling only in the sense that it has to be accommodated to the vision. It would be out of place here, perhaps, and far too technical, to define the difference between such a method as Sargent's and say that of Pre-Raphaelitism. But roughly, the Pre-Raphaelite concentrates on each object. For each object, say in a room, is in turn his subject as he paints that room. The impressionist, Sargent, only has the one subject, that room, the different objects in it explaining themselves only in so far as their surfaces and character are defined in the general impression by the way they take the light—in short, almost an impression as it would be received on a lens. If we remember all this we can appreciate the extreme sensitiveness both of Sargent's vision and touch. For his brush conveys almost with the one touch—so spontaneous in feeling is his work—not only the amount but the shape of the light on any surface. Thus the shapes of everything in the picture are finally resolved, and we might also say without curiosity as to their causes. We are given the impression, which would have been our own impression: since in regard to a portrait, for instance, when we meet a person our curiosity does not immediately extend to such details as the character and number of buttons on his coat. With this method always goes spontaneity, Sargent's pre-eminent gift. He values it so highly that he does not scruple to recommence a picture more than once and carry it through again in the one mood, if in the first instance his art may have miscarried, not permitting himself to doctor up the first attempt. To the constant sense of freshness in his work which such a way of working must imply, I think a great measure of his vogue is to be attributed, though others have coloured more prettily, flattered more, and subordinated themselves to the amiable ambitions of their sitters.

VII

IS it a fancy?—but I see a resemblance between the art of Sargent and that in writing of Mr. Henry James. The same pleasure in nuances of effect in detail, and the readiness to turn to the life at hand for this. To enjoy Sargent is above all to appreciate the means by which he obtains effect in detail, the economy of colour and of brush marks with which he deceives the eye, and the quality of subtle colour in the interpretation of minor phenomena. On the large scale, in the general effect, the quality of his colour is sometimes uninviting. But when at its best it takes the everyday colour of things as if it was colour, without the hysterical exaggeration with which so much youthful contemporary art attempts to cheat itself and other people. If Sargent's admirers do not claim that he sees all the colour there is in things, they claim for him that he sees colour and has the reverence for reality which prevents a tawdry emphasis upon it for the sake of sweetness of effect. And after the sweetmeat vagaries, which have followed in the wake of Whistler, by those without that master's self-control, this is refreshing.

Sargent's brush seems to trifle with things that are trifling, to proceed thoughtfully in its approach to lips and eyes. In painting accessories around his sitters there is the accommodation of touch to the importance of the objects suggested, and nowadays, since interior painting is the fashion—to suit the taste of a young man of genius imposing his peculiar gift upon the time—there are many portraits where the sitter is brought into line with an elaborate setting out of *objets d'art*, the painter's pleasure in the treatment of these manifesting itself sometimes at the sitter's expense. Translating everything by the methods we have described, Sargent preserves throughout his pictures a certain quality of paint. The impression of the characteristic surface of any material is made within this quality, by the responsiveness of his brush to the subtlest modification of effect which differentiates between the nature of one surface and another, as they are influenced by the light upon them at the moment. There are painters who do not translate reality into paint in this way, but who have striven to imitate the surface qualities of objects by varying, imitative ways of applying their paint. Sargent is not this kind of realist.

He is a realist in the sense that Goya, the great Spanish painter of the eighteenth century, was one, for the Spaniard had just such an eagerness to come closer to the sense of life than the close imitation of its outside could bring him. Sargent is more polite, less impetuous, but still it is life as it is, that quickens his brush and informs all his virtuosity. His technique presents life vividly, but presents it to us with a sense of accomplishment in art, the equivalent of the accomplished art of living of the majority of his sitters. I am thinking of a portrait of a lady, and she is turning the leaves of a book, and in the lowered eyes, and the movement of the hand, there is more than arrested movement, there is an expression of an attitude consciously assumed which ordinarily would have been an unconscious one, and so accurate is the painting, that the sitter is detected as it were in this self-consciousness. In portraits of a ceremonial order, for people to sit in a group with a pleasant indispensable air of naturalness, is of course an affair on the artist's part of very thoughtful arrangement. But while composition should not betray the affectation of natural movement, movement must not be conveyed in a merely sensational,

PLATE VI.—LADY ELCHO, MRS. ADEANE, AND LADY TENNANT

(In the collection of the Hon. Percy Wyndham)

A portrait group of the daughters of the Hon. Percy Wyndham. In the background is the famous portrait of Lady Wyndham, mother of the Hon. Percy Wyndham, painted by the late G. F. Watts, O.M.R.A.

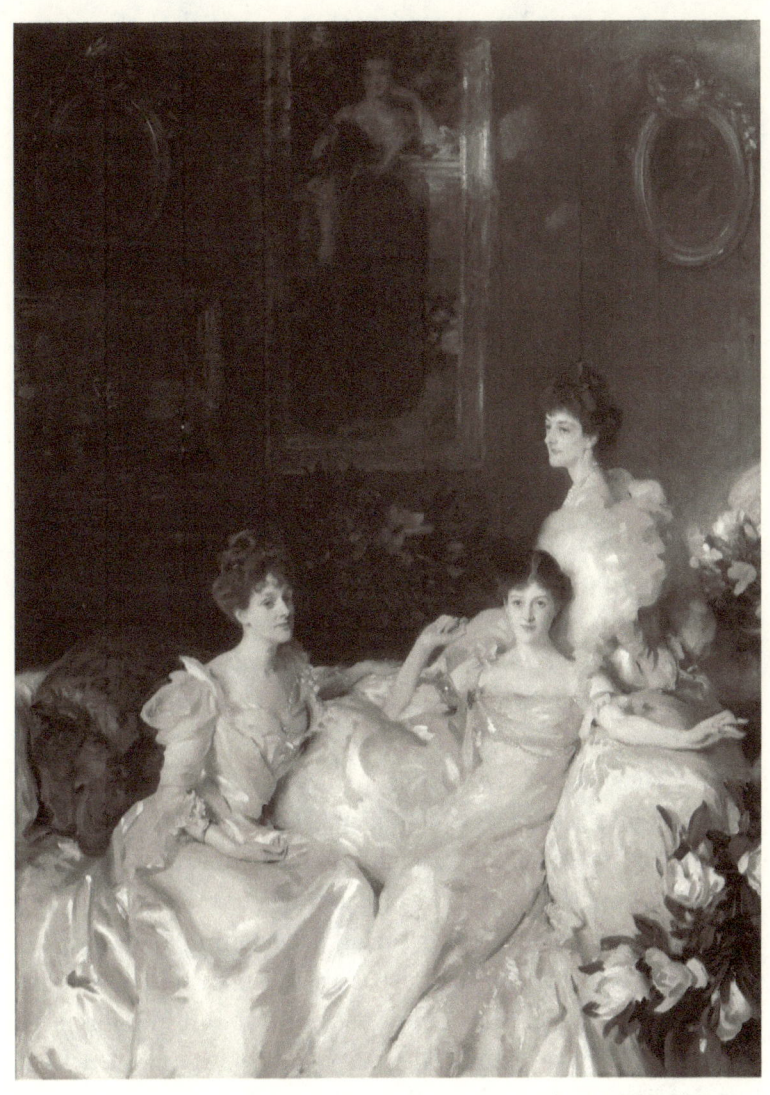

snapshot manner. For the slightest reflection on this matter will betray to us that in the latter pretension we are cheated, since we cannot fail to remember that to complete the canvas the sitter must have recovered the pose day after day, hour after hour, in the studio. Sargent's instincts are so tuned to the appropriate, having the tact which itself is art, that whilst in this kind of portraiture we do not question the grouping or the movement of his sitters as unreal, we do not accept it as quite natural. We instinctively know that in proportion as it is made to look too natural it would be unreal, untrue to the conditions which the painter's art actually encountered. Sargent, who permits nothing to stand between him and nature, will not permit such an inartistic lie to stand between us and the sincerity of his painting. He does not betray us in his love of what is of the moment, by giving us sham of this kind instead of the real thing.

At every point at which we take his art and examine it, the evidence all points to one form of success. The sitters posing are really posing, their action is not even made unnaturally real as we have shown, and in the distances in the room round them, there is the reality of space dividing them from things at the other end of the room. Reality, within the confines of the particular truths to which his method is subject, has been the evident intention all through his art. From this standpoint it often compels admiration in cases where it would have to be withdrawn were we substituting in our mind another ideal, examining his work, for instance, only in the light of a sensitive colour beauty which the painter has not put first and foremost. Some artists have embraced reality only as it justified their imagination. If we look on Sargent's art for anything inward except that which looks through the eyes and determines the smile of his sitter, we shall find our sympathies break down. Unnecessary perhaps to say this, yet it were as well to make quite clear the light in which we should regard the work of an artist who has wholly succeeded in self-expression, the only known form of success in art.

In analysing some men's work, we wish above all to know them, to know the mind that thus environs itself. With others it is their art which tempts us to further and further knowledge of its truths while, as with Shakespeare, the artist behind it becomes impersonal. Thus it is with Sargent's art. It is true that if we wish to know an artist we can never under any circumstances become more intimate with him than in his art, whether we find him in it far away in remote valleys or at the centre of fashionable life. And this though the dreamer may be a man of fashion and the painter of society live a life retired.

Of Sargent's water-colours, much might be said. To some extent they explain his oils, yet he seems to allow himself in them a greater freedom, just as the medium itself is freer than that of oils—more accidental, and the masters of this art control its propensity for accidental effect as its very spirit, guiding it with skill to results which baffle and perplex by the ingenuity with which they give illusion. First, as last, a painter has to accept the fact that he conveys nothing except by illusion; that he can never bring his easel so close to the subject, or his materials to such minuteness of touch, that his art becomes pure imitation; nor can he secure the adjustment of proportion between a large subject and a small panel which would give in every case such imitation. The supreme artist accepts the standpoint first instead of last, and the greater his art becomes, the greater his power in its mysterious control of effect.

VIII

THERE are some painters whose work we may personally wholly dislike—dislike their outlook—even our favourite subjects becoming intolerable to us in their art. It is something in their nature antipathetic to our own. Of course, mediocre work does not assume such proportions in our mind. Then there are painters who, through some affinity of temperament with our own, make everything their art touches pleasant to us. And then there are the impersonal artists, Velazquez, Millais, and Sargent, taking apparently quite an impersonal view of life. Sargent's world is everybody's world, and if we are affected one way or another by it, it is as life affects us.

One has heard a painter say, "I can paint those things because I love them." Judged by his treatment of so many things, of nearly everything, how much must Sargent love life. One man can paint flowers and another marble—Sargent paints everything; and, to paraphrase, almost it might be said that what he doesn't paint isn't worth painting. But all this is nothing if he never penetrates, as Meissonier and others never penetrated, below the surface; if he gave no symbols in his art of things invisible.

We like some of the subjects he has painted, others we dislike so much that we wonder he has painted them; just as in life there are people and surroundings to which we are attracted, and others from whom we keep away.

To the realist by temperament the effect of the details of any scene accepted direct from nature provide exciting inspiration, and he least of all is likely to turn to decorative composition, which, with its resemblance to a form imposed in verse, only aids in the interpretation of the subject in proportion as it is imaginatively inspired. A painter pre-occupied with the opportunities which any incident may offer for the interpretation of subtleties, will often accept any scene from nature and almost any point of view as composition. For the old formulas of composition—of the time when composition was regarded as something to be taught—went with a decorative conception of things, was in itself a form of decoration. And whilst it has been said that all art is decorative, it will perhaps be found that the naturalistic painter is too much excited with incident to scheme much for a rhythmic presentation of it in the frame. Such a canvas as Sargent's "Salmon Fishing in Norway," lately exhibited in the McCulloch collection, a portrait painted in the open, of a youth resting on the bank of a river with caught salmon and tackle beside him, the centre of a skilfully painted piece of landscape, is a case in point. The difficulties which subjects have presented have often seemed Sargent's inspiration in landscape: rocks presenting surfaces to the light with a thousand variations; the wet basins of bronze fountains receiving coloured reflections and the diamond lights in the fountain splashes; grey architecture with its soft shadows, architecture white in the sun with its cool blue shadows, like fragments of night in the doorways. It is this mysterious sensation of light and shadow alternating everywhere, changing the colour of the day itself as the day advances, which Sargent meets. He is one of the few painters who have faced the noon. He has this great command of art's slender resources, and he is matter-of-fact enough to be happy at this uncompromising time of day, unbelieved in by the workers, so inconsiderate to the lazy with its heat. The noon has not many with its praises, and "all great art is praise." Painters have got up at dawn to communicate to us its everyday recurring freshness, as of an eternal spring, and has not evening always been the painter's hour? Sargent has faced the noon, which demands so much sensitiveness that the over-sensitive shrink. His brush has given it in water-colours the finest interpretation it has yet received.

PLATE VII.—THE MISSES WERTHEIMER

(In the collection of Asher Wertheimer, Esq.)

Portraits of the daughters of Asher Wertheimer, Esq., the eminent art-expert. Mr. Wertheimer is himself the subject of one of the best of Sargent's portraits.

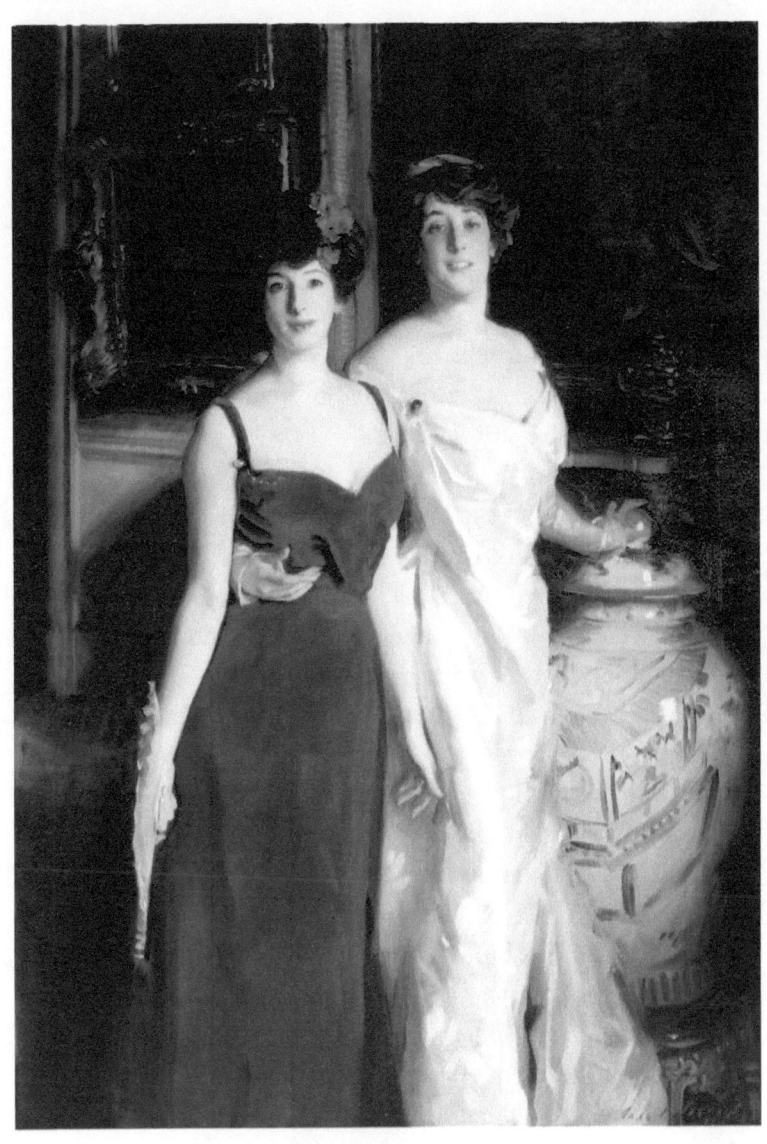

45

IX

TO go back to the matter of composition again. In his portrait groups, where the mere fact that the sitters have to be grouped implies that he is not dealing from the start with an impression direct, we find he is a master of the finest composition, as in his group of Mrs. Carl Meyer and children. And yet to one who will take not one touch with his brush from what is not before him, such a view of his subject must be incalculable in its difficulties.

The painter has never made a passage of painting the excuse for incongruity. The arrangements in his pictures are always probable. It is legitimate in many cases that they should only be imaginatively probable. Any arrangement is probable in a studio, and affording themselves too much licence in this respect some painters wonder why the public are inclined to discredit most of what they do. The logical quality, the sanity of Sargent's art is yet another reason for its vogue; it has not the unreasonableness of studio production, it commends itself to a world that perhaps is not wrong in assuming that the artistic licence is applied for by those who are not sane. Sargent has on occasion had to resort to all sorts of devices to obtain effects and composition that he has desired, but he has always kept faith with the public, and had the true artist's regard for their illusions. He allows his sitters to wear their best clothes, but he never dresses them up; no, to please him they must wholly belong to the life of which they are a part, it is the attitude in which they interest him and all of us. We have then to think of Sargent not only as a painter, but as the maker of human documents—like Balzac, the creator of imperishable characters—with this advantage over Balzac, that all his characters have especially sat to him. It is how posterity will undoubtedly regard this array of brilliant pictures. Of the people they will know nothing but the legend of their actions and Sargent's record of their face. We have undoubtedly felt that when a man of real distinction of mind has worn them, the top hat and cylindrical trouser leg were not so bad. They have indeed, under the influence of personality, seemed on occasions the most august and distinguished garments in the world. But there must come disillusion, the humour of it all will some day dawn, but it will not be before a Sargent picture. He has at any rate immortalised those things, just as Velazquez has made beautiful for ever the outrageous clothes in which his Infantas were imprisoned. We are reconciled to such things in art by the same process as we are in life, in Sargent's case by the unforgettable rendering of the distinction of many of his sitters.

X

IT is the work of the secondary artist that is always perfect—of its sort; for it will not accept its reward, to wit, the finished picture, until the last effort has been expended. With the masters of the first order, it is otherwise. We have said they paint as they think; who but the amateur always thinks at his best? When a man's art has become a part of him, it suffers with his moods. He always works, and his work is always his companion, an indulgence. In his exalted moments it rises to heights by which we estimate his genius, but which sensible criticism does not expect him to live up to, any more than we expect a brilliant conversationalist always to be equally brilliant. This is why a master's work is always so interesting. That it has become so flexible an expression of his own nature is its charm, if we really regard it as art, and do not look upon the artist as a manufacturer who must be reliable, who having once turned out of his workshop a work of surpassing perfection, must be expected to keep to that standard or be classed with the defaulting tradesman whose goods do not come up to his sample. A painter makes or mars his own reputation by the care or carelessness of his work, but it is his own work, and he is not under any obligation to us to keep it up to a certain standard if it does not interest him to sacrifice everything for that standard. Sargent's work has been splendidly unequal. Sometimes it has been disillusioned, tired, at other times all his energy has seemed gathered up into a *tour de force*. An intensity there is about Sargent's earlier work which we cannot find in some of his later pictures, sureness of itself has brought freedom and with it freedom's qualities, which we must take pleasure in for their own sake.

It is frequently enough the weakness of painters to return constantly in their art to some particular gesture or arrangement in which their mastery is complete. This has not been the case with Sargent; instead, his mastery has completed itself only through a constant encounter with new difficulties.

A quality of all great art is reticence, something which will never let the master, to whom it is not disastrous to be careless, be so; for carelessness nearly always means over-statement, and exaggeration. Ah! just the qualities if a work of art is to arrest attention in a modern exhibition. A common question at the Royal Academy is "Where are the Sargents?" by some enthusiastic visitor who has passed them several times. No, Sargent's victories do not startle, winged victories do not, but advertisements do.

PLATE VIII.—MRS. A. L. LANGMAN

(In the collection of A. L. Langman, Esq., C.M.G.)

A portrait of the wife of A. L. Langman, Esq., C.M.G., who served with the Langman Field Hospital, in connection with the equipment of which for the South African War his father, Sir John Langman, Bart., is remembered.

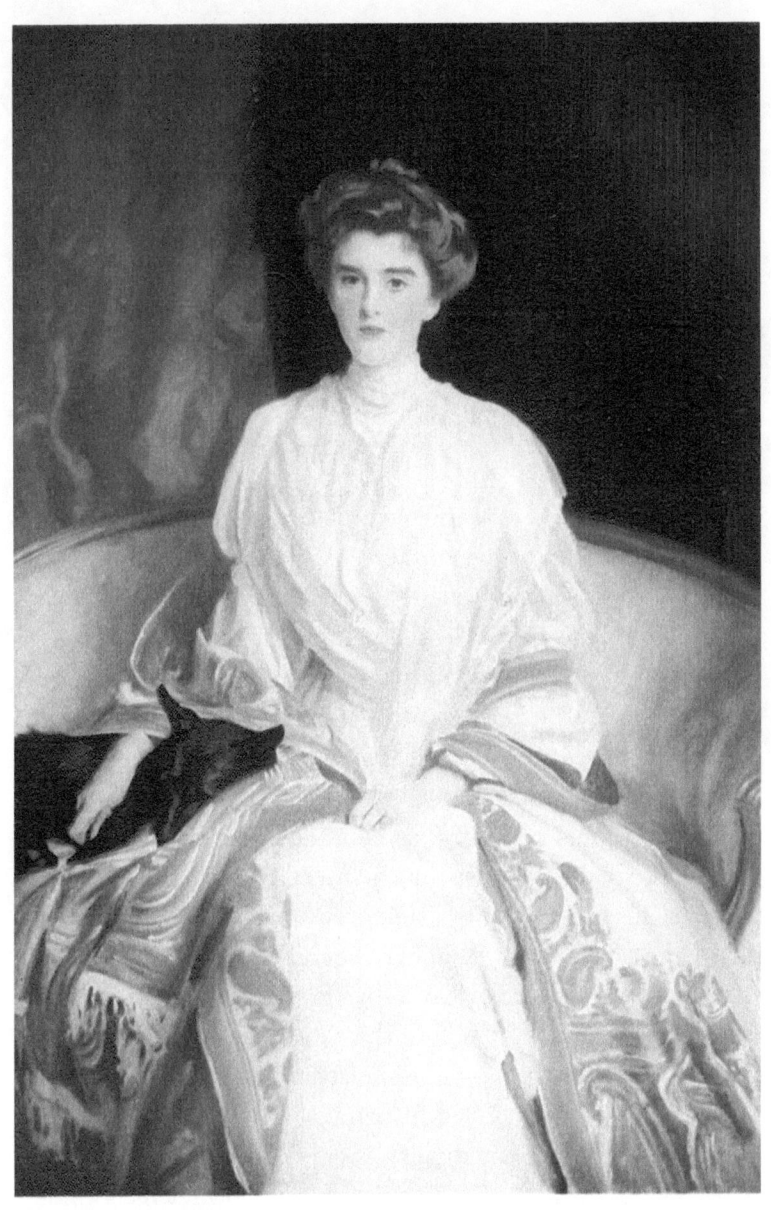

XI

SARGENT was born of American parents in Florence in 1856, and passed his boyhood there. No art, it would seem at first, is further away than his from all the Florentine traditions, and yet in the decorative colour values, which give distinction to his finest works, he is the child of Florence. The Renaissance attitude towards life itself was highly imaginative, so into visionary art reality was carried. Consulting the origin of all their visions, the Florentines returned imaginatively to what was real. It is the beauty of reality which is the fervour of their great designs, and as a humanist, Sargent is their descendant.

When, at the age of nineteen, he came to Paris, he was already, we are told, an artist of promise, and he went to Carolus Duran with youth's conscious, ardent necessity of embracing a fresh view of the world altogether. The lighter touch of Carolus Duran, the worldly painting, the lively art of things living, if a superficial art, was refreshing, no doubt, to one accustomed only to the beautiful memories of ardour expressed five centuries before. And superficiality, demoralising to the superficial, could only give some added swiftness to a brush inclined to halt with too much intensity whilst life, its one enthusiasm, was racing by. He never experimented under Carolus Duran. He was beginning that unerring sensitiveness of painting, which is only learnt by drudgery, the almost luxuriously easy virtuosity, before the acquirement of which, complete freedom of expression cannot begin, or sympathy declare itself as from a well-played instrument.

An artist with individuality is careless of asserting it, and it is perhaps just the one thing in the world which cannot but assert itself. Those who strive for originality through the unaccustomed may without hesitation be put down as those who are without confidence in their own nature. The individuality of Sargent, as striking as any in his day, is unselfconsciously expressed. If we could strain from a work of art the self-conscious, which is always the unnatural element, all that ever gave it any force would still be left in it. Submitted to this test, how much so-called originality would crumble, while the individualism of Sargent still remained.

When leaving the studio of Carolus Duran, he painted a portrait of that painter, a summing, as it were, of all he owed to him before he courted another influence. He went to Madrid, there to study the living elements of art in the school of a dead master, Velazquez, in whose life encompassing art nothing has gone out of fashion—no, not even the farthingale which the children wear. It was early in the eighties that the Spanish visit ended and Sargent worked in Paris, already a man of note, for the Carolus Duran portrait had been followed by "Portrait of a Young Lady," exhibited in 1881, and "En route pour la Pêche" and "Smoke of Ambergris." In 1882 he exhibited the *tour de force* "El Jaleo," the sensation of the season, and immediately afterwards the "Portraits of Children"—the four children in a dimly-lighted hall, one of the most well-remembered of his pictures of that time. Then came the wonderful "Madame Gautreau." Paris was his headquarters but his visits to England were frequent, and they grew more frequent as the time went on and as his reputation grew in London. It was about half-a-dozen years after the Spanish visit that he came to this country to live here permanently and make his art our own. He was elected an Associate of the Royal Academy in 1894, a Royal Academician in 1897.

XII

WE should say something of Sargent's influence on contemporary art, which has been immense. It has been thought that, deceived by the brilliance of his results, with their great air of spontaneity, younger painters have been led astray. This, we believe, is a mistake. The weakest go to the wall, but it is probable that the example of Sargent has succeeded in lifting the whole standard of painting in the country, bringing—even the great incompetent, within measuring distance of a useful ideal; an ideal of sympathy disciplined with every touch, and an ideal of difficult things. Is not Art always difficult? It has been so to Sargent, with everything at his fingers' ends; with everything so much at his fingers' ends that under special circumstances he once completed a life-size three-quarter length portrait in a single day. He was in America, and had promised to paint the portrait. The sittings were put off, and at last the friend who was to sit was suddenly called away; but Sargent came with his materials in the morning, and the sitter gave him the day. They were probably both nearly dead at the end of it, but a large finished painting had been begun and ended.

Sargent's countrymen have appreciated every manifestation of his gifts. Lately he exhibited eighty-three of his watercolours in Brooklyn. He will not part with them singly. Brooklyn enthusiastically bought the whole collection for its Art Museum.

Fame has not spoilt his retiring nature, and even by his art a barrier is raised, in front of which the master will not show himself, but I hope it is an intimacy that we have established with him in his art. Mine is but the privilege of murmuring the introduction, and any charges to be brought against me must be laid at Sargent's door. For a great artist creates not only his art, but that which it inspires. This is indeed the mysterious province of artistic creation; the artist creating beyond his art that which comes into our minds through contact with it; so framing our thoughts and setting in motion waves infinitely continued in the thoughts that pass through every man to his companions.

www.ingramcontent.com/pod-product-compliance
Lightning Source LLC
Chambersburg PA
CBHW020711180526
45163CB00008B/3032